Simple Internet Safety

The Knowledge You Need to Avoid Being Scammed on the Internet

2016 Edition

Michael Paulhus

Introduction

Back in 2012 my mother called me up to tell me something had happened to her computer. It so happened that my father was surfing web sites and suddenly the computer locked up with a blue screen and a warning that they had been on illegal websites and that if they did not send the FBI (really some criminals) one thousand dollars in bit coin (online currency explained later), that they would never be able to use their computer again wiping it completely. My mother called me in tears my father cursing and swearing in the background ready to go deposit money to send to the criminal's money. They had been victims of the Ransom Scam (explained later).

Luckily my Mom has me for a son and I was able to fix her problem without her losing money to scammers. I blocked some sites had them get a better anti-virus and a VPN, advised them on what to look out for and I felt better, at ease knowing Mom and Dad were safe from the cyber criminals.

I became aware that many people do not know what to look out for and what precautions to take to avoid being scammed on the internet.

I knew I had to teach whoever I could on how to avoid scams. Some people are so very afraid of being scammed, especially if they have already been scammed before and are suffering from the embarrassment and feeling of being victimized. I assure you if you just read this book and absorb what I share and use some common sense you will be fine.

It is a very frightening and embarrassing thing to be scammed and the fear of being scammed on the internet is a valid one. In 2014 there were 123,684 complaints about scams to the IC3, the FBI's Internet Crime Complaint Center, and since its inception in 2007 to 2014 there have been a total of 3,175,611 reports. The IC3 reported in 2014 that the amount of money scammed from these complaints is an enormous sum, $800,492,073 to be exact and that is just 2014 alone. These numbers don't include all of the scams that go unreported to the IC3 year after year estimated to be in the millions of scams and the billions of dollars.

Florida residents especially seniors seem to be the primary target victim for scammers. As the FBI reported in 2014 Florida was the second only to California in money stolen through scams. Floridians were taken for a total of 52,544,107 and those aged 50+ were the highest number of complaints losing a total of $31,641,070 almost three quarters of all the money scammed in the entire state.

The threat is real and growing every day. With the popularity of social media, it has fast become a popular platform for criminals. The affordability and convenience of cellphones and tablets have fast made them a common accessory putting people online now more than ever. People now surf the web while riding the bus or walking their dog, there is almost no escape from the internet these days.

The extreme convenience of the internet makes life easier and communicating with our friends and family is a sinch keeping us in contact like never before. Though the downfall of living In a world where text messaging and ordering your sandwich on an app are as common as making a phone call, we are more vulnerable to cyber criminals than ever before.

There are so many ways that criminals can get your personal and financial information using the internet. With what I teach you in this book you should know enough to keep from being scammed and afford to surf the web using the latest technology with the utmost confidence.

Knowledge is power and I know many of you that are purchasing this book are not tech savvy and that's why I have broken the information down simply and without too much technical jargon. I don't want you to be intimidated by this book or frightened by what it teaches you, I want you to use it as a tool to keep you safe while online.

You will learn not only how to avoid being scammed online, but also the terms and terminology the criminals and law enforcement use when referring to the types of crimes committed online. Don't let the term Doxing or Pharming scare you away from the knowledge of what they mean and how it can affect you. It is all defined for you here your little book of simple internet safety.

My hope is by you reading this book that it helps ease your mind and gives you the confidence to enjoy the internet with the knowledge of how scams happen and how to avoid them and so much more valuable information.

Chapter 1

Choosing Anti-Virus Software

Your first line of defense on the web, is your antivirus software. Your antivirus software will protect you from a lot. The three things your antivirus defends your computer against are:

Malware - software that is intended to damage or disable computers and computer systems.

Spyware - software that enables a user to obtain covert information about another's computer activities by transmitting data covertly from their hard drive.

Viruses – malicious code that is capable of copying itself and typically has a detrimental effect, such as corrupting the system or destroying data.

Many viruses can be installed just by going to a site or clicking media file such as a banner and this can happen to anyone, even this guy. That's where your antivirus comes in. Think of it like your castle walls when it comes to being online. A good antivirus will stop the virus before you even download it, blocking the page of the link before you ever see the link in some cases. Here is where I must say always listen to your antivirus! If it says something is unsafe there is a reason for that, don't ignore those warnings.

A lot of people ask me what is the best antivirus out there and if you do a little research you will find that all antivirus software brands say they are the best. So how do you choose a good one? Do you use the antivirus that came with your device? Do you use a free antivirus? Well you will be happy to know that there are antivirus testing organizations out there and they test these antivirus software brands every couple of months. They test them so much due to the constantly changing viruses on the internet. Thanks to these great independent organizations, you don't have to choose an antivirus blindly; you can make an informed decision.

The first thing you need to decide is whether to use a free antivirus or shell out the clams for a paid antivirus. Believe it or not there are many solid antiviruses out there that are completely free. Granted a lot of this free antivirus protection software does just as it's titled stop viruses. They detect and block malware and spyware. The free antivirus programs lack the full security suite with features like firewall, anti-theft, anti-spam granted these features are not exactly necessary they are nice to have. Also the free products tend to nag you about purchasing an upgrade, but that's how these companies make money. You will find though that the paid antivirus programs are the easiest to use and perform the best. The paid versions tend to be the highest graded in the tests by the independent testing companies. I will tell you that I personally use a paid antivirus now, but I have used free versions in the past.

Free or paid most importantly use an antivirus with a good reputation and avoid using obscure unheard of products. Reputable well-known companies are subject to the testing mentioned earlier and the smaller companies are not, so therefore they may not protect you against the latest threats. Another risk of choosing an unknown antivirus brand is that scammers are known to disguise malware as an antivirus so by downloading this "fake antivirus" you are in fact downloading a virus. Some names used by fake software are Antivirus Live, Antivirus Remover and Internet Security 2012.

Most importantly check the tests. The tests will tell you how successful each brand was at blocking the malware samples given to them, as well as how well they performed and how easy they are to use.

Here are a couple sites where you can find the recent test ratings of popular antivirus software:

Virus Bulletin Magazine - www.virusbulletin.com – Virus Bulletin is a regular independent comparative and certification system. They test bi-monthly and grade the performance of the antivirus tested and how it scored in performance and reliability.

AV Test – www.av-test.org – AV Test is another good independent comparative and certification testing site. Though they only test three times a year they have a very easy to follow grading system. AV Test uses a simple grading system for Protection, Performance and Usability.

Chapter 2

Safe Wi-Fi

First let us discuss what Wi-Fi (Wireless Fidelity) is. Wi-Fi is a wireless networking technology that allows computers and other devices to communicate over a wireless signal.

Wi-Fi is the standard way computers connect to wireless networks. Nearly all modern computers have built-in Wi-Fi chips that allows users to find and connect to wireless routers.

A router is a device that routes your internet signal wirelessly from your modem. The modem is the device that connects to your cable wire or phone jack providing you access to the internet.

What we will be discussing in this chapter is public Wi-Fi in chapter 6 we discuss how to keep your home router safe. In this chapter we discuss keeping you safe on a network that is not your own.

The internet is now portable thanks to phones, laptops and tablets and with this portability comes the risk of connecting to Wi-Fi that is not your own. There are ways scammers can steal your information from your devices when you use public Wi-Fi and that's why it is important to exercise extreme caution when connecting to public Wi-Fi.

Scammers can intercept your data using a **man-in-the-middle attack.** The scammer sets up a network called "free Wi-Fi" or copies the name of a real free Wi-Fi network to make you think you are on a legitimate network.

For example, some friends of mine were on vacation and were checked into a hotel. These friends of mine they do a lot of business online selling via a popular online store. So on vacation, they were at the hotel, it was rainy and they were bored they decided to check their sales while they were away. SO they log onto the Wi-Fi named for their hotel. Upon logging onto the internet a page prompts them to enter their room number, "seems legit". They logged into their store account, checked their bank account balance, answered some email and logged off and got on with their rainy vacation.

Talk about a bad vacation, not only did it rain all week, but when they returned home they found that their bank account had been emptied, had been locked out of their own store and email account. It took them a while to realize what happened, they had been the victims of a **man-in-the-middle attack**. When they logged into the apparent hotel Wi-Fi they were actually logging through a scammers network probably located in one of the rooms nearby and using a sniffer which intercepted all of the information they entered on the web sites.

Sniffers are network monitors also known as snoops or network probes. It is software or firmware that monitors data flowing over network links. Originally designed for use by network engineers today hackers and scammers exploit this technology to steal people's information.

To stop something like this from happening to you my first suggestion would be to use your phones cellular data most popularly named 3G or 4G to go online. It is simple enough to activate just turn off your phones Wi-Fi and it should automatically turn on the phones cellular data to get onto the internet. Though this method is very slow even more so when dealing with a lot of data and it is not 100% safe as someone could still intercept you through a fake cell tower though that is an extremely rare thing to happen.

If you really must use public Wi-Fi the first thing you should do is check what the name of the network is with a staff member that works at the place you are trying to receive Wi-Fi. If my friends would have checked with their hotel they would have found out that the hotels Wi-Fi was down that whole week. Also most public Wi-Fi networks today require some sort of password as a security measure.

And before you get online using public Wi-Fi make sure that you aren't publicly sharing your computers files. If you are using a **Windows** laptop go to your Advanced Sharing Settings and be sure that you turn off file and printer sharing. On **Mac** computers open system preferences navigate to the sharing icon and unclick the check box next to file sharing.

If you are online a lot in public places you may consider getting and using a **VPN,** I will talk a lot about VPN's in this book as it is a great way to keep your browsing sessions safe from unwanted eyes. VPN stands for Virtual Private Network. A VPN encrypts internet traffic from your device to the server making it near impossible for scammers to get your information using Sniffers by masking your IP address.

The iOS devices (iPhones) have integrated VPN servers where Android users must use a third party app. iOS users can turn on a VPN in the general settings. One option for Android users is an app called Secure Wireless which automatically detects unsecured Wi-Fi and activates a VPN where needed or TunnelBear which works really well and even has a decent free version; both apps are available in the Google Play store.

Another way to keep your info safe is enable two-factor authentication wherever available. This is where a site will ask you to keep your cell phone number on file. When an unknown device tries to log into your account these sites will text you a code that you must enter before continuing, so if you are sniffed it will at least keep some of your information safe and keep you not locked out of your email.

Remember to always remove networks from your trusted network list. This will stop your device from automatically using networks scammers have set up imitating real public Wi-Fi spots. Tell your device to forget the network. This means that your phone or PC won't automatically connect again to the network if you're in range. You can do this by unchecking

"Connect automatically when this network is in range" in Windows Network and Sharing Center. On Mac in system preferences then Network uncheck "Remember networks this computer has joined."

Finally, and most importantly be mindful of what you do on public Wi-Fi don't check your bank account balance or log into your online store. The safest thing to do is wait until you are using cellular data or your home Wi-Fi before you log into sensitive sites.

Chapter 3

Email Safety

Communication is ever changing and one of the most popular ways to communicate today is via email. Since the beginning of the internet scammers have preyed on victims through emails. Fake emails are very common and sadly, it's because many of us are the unsuspecting, all too willing to believe in freebies, prizes, and distress calls.

Being able to spot a fake email is important to avoid becoming a victim and by reporting these emails to the proper authorities you are being a good citizen and helping prevent others without the knowledge from falling victim as well. **You should report all hoax emails and other online scams to** www.IC3.gov this website is easily found at the back of this book along with many others to keep handy.

Email hoaxes are often called **"Phishing"** attempts. This is what they call it when a scammer sends out a mass email to a list of addresses he has managed to obtain through other scams, hackers or other illegal methods.

The scammer hopes that at least a few of the people on this list will be gullible enough to respond by sending cash or personal details about themselves.

Basically a phishing scammer wants your money or information that can give them access to sources of your money. They use methods to try and trick you into revealing sensitive information about you such as your passwords, Social Security numbers, mother's maiden name, account numbers, date of birth amongst many other identifying information. Phishing scams can also happen via social media sites which we will discuss later in this book.

Here is a list of red flags to beware of to help you avoid being a victim of a hoax email:

🚩 **Bad Spelling:** If an email is supposedly from some official source the first red flag should be bad spelling and/or grammar. Corporations and other professionals pay people to edit their correspondence and so there should rarely be any misspelled words or bad grammar.

🚩 **Unsolicited Requests:** If you have never heard of the company or person emailing you be suspicious. If an email refers to signing up to or registering for their site/service and you don't recall doing so it is probably a scam.

Too Good to Be True: If the email is full of promises of some great reward or inheritance it probably really is too good to be true. Also if someone is being very personal and you don't know them it is most likely a scam.

Free Money for Information: Beware any email that offers you money for information. Be very wary of any offer of money for your personal information.

Request for Money: Asking you for money should always be a red flag, even if it appears to be from someone that you know. Scammers prey on our need to care for our loved ones so if you suddenly get an email from your child traveling abroad saying they have lost all of their belongings and need you to send them money be wary and use other sources to verify the information. This is not uncommon as hackers can gain access to your personal emails and find information to try and convince you they are someone you know. When in doubt a phone call is your best recourse as scammers have yet to be able to steal your loved ones' voice to use against you.

Other Countries: If an email comes to you from somewhere you don't live, like China or Australia and you don't know anybody there it is most likely a phishing attempt.

Chain Emails: Always bear in mind that your friends and colleagues can have their emails hacked and the sender may not be your friend but a scammer instead. It is important to not forward chain emails yourself to avoid spreading a scam and also it is illegal in some countries and is definitely bad etiquette.

Wire Transfers: So your good friend of many years emails you and tells you that they have been robbed and need money to pay for their plane ticket home, you offer to buy a ticket directly from the airline and they refuse and insist on a wire transfer, you can bet on the fact that you are being scammed. Avoid sending money via wire transfer always confirm either face to face or on the phone with the person you are sending it to and involve financial or legal representatives to ensure its legitimacy.

Information Requests: If you ever get an email from a company or website that you do actually do business with that asks you for any personal information, information that they should already have or insists that you have to follow a link, do not respond and do not click any links. Do not use any phone number in the email. Do not copy and paste that address into your browser either. Close the email open a new browser window and go to the companies site by manually typing the address into the browser and contact them directly through their website to inquire about the email. Remember that banks do not send emails asking for personal information from an email link go to the bank in person or call a number (not from the email) to talk to a representative.

Threats: You have done nothing wrong. If you feel threatened, do not worry. A threat of immediate detrimental action if you don't respond with personal information are illegitimate, they do not deserve your attention, but may need to be drawn to the attention of police. Contact the police, anti-scam authorities immediately.

Using these red flags as a guideline you should be able to avoid most email hoaxes, but keep in mind scammers can be quite cunning and clever when it comes to attacking you via email. Trust your gut instinct if it doesn't feel right it probably isn't.

When checking your email be sure you are awake alert and sober. Not only will your mental reflexes be less than optimal, you're more likely to fall for sob stories and great deals when you're not clear headed.

Most importantly never let feelings of guilt or fear force you into responding to an email. Not following that charity link does not make you a bad person and subpoenas and court documents always come in the regular post office mail. Government agencies do not send unsolicited e-mails and debt collectors will contact you via phone not email.

Remember to pass on any information about hoax emails you may come across to your friends and family to help them avoid getting phished as well. Only by working together can we stop scammers and prevent others from becoming victims of email hoaxes.

Chapter 4

Randsomware

In case you have never heard of Ransomware or the Internet Ransom Scam you should know it is a nasty malware (type of computer virus) that locks up your system and threatens to not restore it to extort money from you.

Ransomware is becoming frighteningly more common and is almost always insidious, difficult to remove, and, in many cases, expensive.

Often the users My Documents folder and libraries are locked and often encrypted. Upon the locking of these files the scammers message is displayed informing the user of the price that must be paid to regain access to the computer. Yep they make you pay for your own files!

Data isn't only locked, however; in some cases, the user is accused of being a pedophile, using illegal images and a message purporting to be from a known law enforcement agency. In 2013, McAfee revealed it had collected in excess of 250,000 ransomware samples, each unique, in the first quarter of that year alone.

The best way to avoid Ransomware is to stick to websites you know and trust and when on new web sites do not click any links. Having a good antivirus as discussed in Chapter 1 is the best offense against this malware. Also important is to have a pop-up blocker seeing a lot of Ransomware is delivered through popups.

Avoid downloads from unknown sources or web sites you do not completely trust. Last but certainly not least, it is vital to back up not only your personal computer files very regularly, but your system files as well.

If you do find yourself a victim of Ransomware, remember the following:

• The warnings are fake and have no association with any legitimate authorities. The message just uses images and logos of legal institutions to make the it look authentic.

• Do not pay the ransom. There is absolutely no guarantee that paying the ransom will give you access to your files again. Handing over the ransom will most likely just make you a target for more malware and scams. If you are reading this too late and you have already paid then you should contact your bank and your local authorities, such as the police immediately. If you paid with a credit card, your bank may be able to block the transaction and return your money.

• Some ransomware will also encrypt or delete the backup versions of your files. This means that even if you have backed up your files and you have set the backup location to be a network or local drive your backups might also be encrypted. Backups on a removable drive, or a drive that wasn't connected when you were infected with the ransomware, might still work.

Getting your files back is tricky but possible, though before you can free the hostage (your computer) you need to eliminate the hostage taker. Follow these steps:

1. **System Restore:** Roll Windows back in time. Doing so doesn't affect your personal files, but it does return system files and programs to the state they were in at a certain time. The System Restore feature must be enabled beforehand; Windows enables it by default. To try a System, Restore, shut down your PC and locate the F8 key on your PC's keyboard. Turn the PC on, and as soon as you see anything on the screen, press the F8 key repeatedly. This

action should bring up the Advanced Boot Options menu; there, select *Repair Your Computer* and press Enter. Next you'll likely have to log on as a user; select your Windows account name. (If you don't have a password set, leave that blank.) Once logged on, you'll find shortcuts to a few tools; click the *System Restore* tool. If System Restore doesn't help and you still can't get into Windows to remove the ransomware, try running a virus scanner from a bootable disc or USB drive; some people refer to this approach as an offline virus scan. If this does work continue to the next step.

2. **Enter Safe Mode:** Entering safe mode is a lot like doing a system restore in step 1. As before shut down your PC and locate the F8 key on your PC's keyboard. Turn the PC on, and as soon as you see anything on the screen, press the F8 key repeatedly. And from the advanced boot menu select *Safe Mode*. In this mode, only the minimum required programs and services are loaded. If any malware is set to load automatically when Windows starts, entering in this mode may prevent it from doing so.

3. **Delete Temporary Files:** Now that you're in Safe Mode, you'll want to run a virus scan. But before you do that, delete your temporary files. Doing this may speed up the virus scanning, free up disk space, and even get rid of some malware. To use the Disk Cleanup utility included with Windows, select *Start*, *All Programs* (or just *Programs*), *Accessories*, *System Tools*, *Disk Cleanup.*

4. **Download and Run a Malware Scanner:** If you already have an antivirus program active on your computer, you should use a different scanner for this malware check, since your current antivirus software may have not detected the malware. Unlike an antivirus program like discussed in chapter 1 an on-demand scanner, searches for malware infections when you open the program manually and run a scan. You should have only one real-time antivirus program installed at a time, but you can keep a few on-demand scanners handy to run scans with multiple programs, thereby ensuring that you're covered.

5. **Recover Your Files if Windows is Corrupted:** This step is optional and is

only necessary if you can't seem to remove the malware or if Windows isn't working properly, you may have to reinstall Windows. Before wiping your hard drive though, be sure to copy all of your files to an external USB or flash drive. If you check your email with a client program (such as Outlook or Windows Mail), make sure that you export your settings and messages to save them. Now that you have backed up everything, reinstall Windows either from the disc that came with your PC or by using your PC's factory restore option, if it has one. As when accessing System Restore or Safe Mode, you must press a certain key on the keyboard in order for the system restore screen to load. If you have a factory restore option, your computer should show you what key to press in the first few seconds after you turn it on; it's usually an F key located along the top of most keyboards.

Chapter 5

Don't Get Doxed

Anonymity is a wonderful thing especially on the internet. On the web you are free to post your views, opinions, rants and even sometimes your personal stories online with the illusion that your real identity is safe and the world could never find out that you are really catlover69.

Notice how I use the word illusion when referring to your safe identity. You should know that more and more of your life is stored in databases, on servers and on social networking sites. Nowadays, it doesn't take much personal details to obtain even more information on someone. Once the puzzle has been put together, someone has your name, address, Social Security number, and more! This person has now Doxed you.

Once you have been Doxed the attacker can then open loans in your name, ruin your credit, and many things in-between. In some cases, completely ruining someone's life.

Doxing is the internet slang term for a type of identity theft. It takes a lot of work to Dox someone and the easier it is to Dox you the better the chances of it happening to you. It could be the result of some internet banter be it political or otherwise that turns heated and some insults are exchanged. You get tired go to bed and forget about it. The next thing you know you're getting pizzas delivered you didn't order, your bank accounts emptied and are being delivered strange packages. Finding yourself the confused new owner of a pet Llama, you may never recover from this kind of attack. Know how to avoid being Doxed.

Avoid Social Media: The first place an attacker goes to gather information on you is Social Media sites like Facebook. You can now use Social Media to sign up for most websites and Facebook even requires you use the name you go by in real life. There is a lot of information about you on just one website when you use Social Media. An attacker can find out who your friends are, who your close friends are, where you work along with a map to its location and even who you are dating or married to. Big deal, you say?

Well I'll tell you a pretty big deal when you click on the "forgot password" button on your banks website what are the questions they ask you, 'where were you born 'what your favorite color is 'your favorite sports team. The attacker can use the information they gather from Social Media to get this information. Don't belive me ask an FBI agent. The Feds use the same technique to profile people during investigations.

If you really must use Social Media use a fake name and an email address for that sole purpose. I know it seems extreme cutting off social media but it really is the best step to staying safe.

Get More Email Addresses: So much today is tied to your email address from your Skype and Netflix accounts to your bank account updates and it amazes me that so many people have everything tied to just one email address.

Seeing how most sites use your email address as a login, when an attacker gets your email address he now knows your login for all of those web sites. If you want to avoid being tracked down use a string of email addresses.

Use a VPN: It makes it so much harder to track your internet activity if your IP address is masked, always use a **VPN** whenever you can.

Search Yourself: Go to a search site like www.pipl.com and search your email address and phone number and see what you find and trace it back to the source. This is a great way to know what information is easily out there about you and where that information is coming from so you can take steps to hide that information.

The last bit of advice I can give to avoid being Doxed is use common sense. Things are only free online because you are being sold. Your habits your likes your dislikes all being sold and inherently such systems fall victim to stealing of massive amounts of personal information. Be aware of what sites you give your email addresses to and make sure no private information is available and if it is remove it.

If you find out that you have been Doxed do not react to your attacker. Don't react, ever. Don't acknowledge it. Don't taunt. Don't say they have the wrong information. **Alert the proper Authorities and Financial Institutions Immediately.**

Chapter 6

Pharming & Protecting your Router

We talked about Phishing in Chapter 3 and in this chapter we will talk about Pharming. Phishing is usually used in conjunction with Pharming as the scammer sends out phishing emails with the intention to luring you to a Pharming site. A Pharming site is a site that a scammer or hacker sets up to look very realistically like a legitimate web site by using your own router against you and then emptying your bank account with that information without you even knowing.

Pharming sites are usually designed to resemble banking web sites. In some cases, victims are sent emails from what looks like a legitimate bank and in these emails is a link and instead of directing them to the banks site so they could log in, the link actually delivers a code to the victim's router using a brute force entry method of common username and password combinations.

Once the code, a malicious type of JavaScript, has succeeded it compromises the victim's router and reconfigures traffic via the internet. The compromised router will then redirect the victim to a phishing site instead of their banks site even when they manually type in the address. The victim will even be directed to the fake site when they attempt to use a search engine. It's some pretty scary stuff considering it does not only effect the computer you were phished on, but any device on your home network and the victim usually has no idea it's happening until the damage is done.

The best way to avoid being Pharmed is by reading Chapter 3 and not clicking the original link, but we are human and prone to mistakes so prevention is key here.

Your internet service provider (ISP) will often offer you a wireless router with your internet service, I highly recommend buying your own. The router that your ISP gives you will have a common preset username and passwords. The issue with home routers using common credentials is that makes it easier for hackers to exploit and gain access to your computer and all other devices in your network.

Purchase your own router or edit the ISP's routers username and password to something you do not use anywhere online.

Some ISP's allow you to change your username and password. You should always change the username and password on ALL routers once you receive them.

 Start by collecting your login information (IP address, username and password for router). This is typically found in router's user manual or on the back of the router itself. An internal IP (Internet Protocol) address consists of 8 numbers separated by dots (*example* 192.168.0.1) the internal IP address is used to uniquely identify your computer on a network. The default internal IP address for most router manufacturers is 192.168.0.1 or 192.168.1.1

I strongly advise you to change this number in the settings and keep it written down somewhere safe. You can retrieve it later if you lose it, by using your computers **command prompt** type the word **ipconfig** then press enter.

In a browser, enter the routers internal IP address into the Address Bar and login with the username and password you found in the manual, command prompt or behind the router. From the routers page after you log on you can change the username and password; usually these settings are under a tab named security though this differs depending on the brand of router you have.

By changing your IP address, username and password for router you should be pretty safe from Pharming. Keep in mind though that hackers are constantly changing their methods and improving their malicious coding. It is best to practice safe emailing at all times to avoid becoming a victim of these types of attacks.

Chapter 7

The Romance Con

Con artists have been a bit glorified by Hollywood over the years; The debonair bachelor or elegant bachelorette, swindling rich men and women out of their fortunes by swooning them romantically.

The Romance Con of Hollywood may make good entertainment on the silver screen, but the real Romance Cons are a lot less delightful and the victims are more often lonely people barely getting by not richer than life billionaires on the Rio Grande.

The real Romance Cons involve scammers pretending to seek companionship or romance online. The criminals search dating sites, chat rooms and social media web sites for personally identifiable information and use well-rehearsed scripts to attract their victims.

The largest reported group of people victimized according to the FBI's 2014 IC3 report was women over the age of 40 making up more than 80% of all victims for a total of $68,529,135.

The victims are told a sob story of some personal tragedy or hardship that has befallen them in order to solicit money from the victim. At times they will carry on an online only relationship with a person for many months before the tragedy strikes making it seem more convincing to the victim by using their earned false sense of trust against them.

Honestly the best way of avoiding this con is **not pursuing a long distance relationship online** in the first place. Keeping your online dating local and avoiding people that are out of your area is the first step to avoiding these scams.

When it comes to dating sites you should **always join a paid site** and only communicate with other paid members seeing credit cards are on file and they actually have to pay to be on the site you are less likely to be scammed. Remember though there are less scammers, but they are still there.

Never ever give any personal information to anyone you've only met online, save getting personal until you meet face to face.

Never open any attachments strangers may send you through email or social media and never click any links they may send you as they could be attempting to send you malicious code or viruses.

Mostly importantly **use common sense** and don't fall for any sob stories. Always be suspicious, there is always a chance the stranger you met online is trying to scam you.

KEEP THIS BOOK BY YOUR COMPUTER!

The threat is real and growing every day. With the popularity of social media, it has fast become a popular platform for criminals. The affordability and convenience of cellphones and tablets have fast made them a common accessory putting people online now more than ever. People now surf the web while riding the bus or walking their dog, there is almost no escape from the internet these days.

The extreme convenience of the internet makes life easier and communicating with our friends and family is a sinch keeping us in contact like never before. Though the downfall of living In a world where text messaging and ordering your sandwich on an app are as common as making a phone call, we are more vulnerable to cyber criminals than ever before.

Michael Paulhus brings you this collection of vital knowlege on how to stay safe while on the internet.

ISBN 9781539748731

9 781539 748731